Martin Heidegger's Grouch

Martin Heidegger's Grouch

Narrated by
Yan Marchand

Illustrated by
Matthias Arégui

Translated by
Anna Street

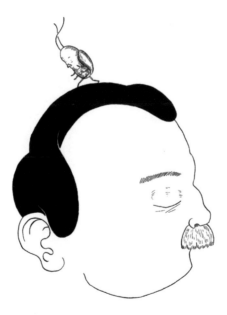

Plato & Co.
diaphanes

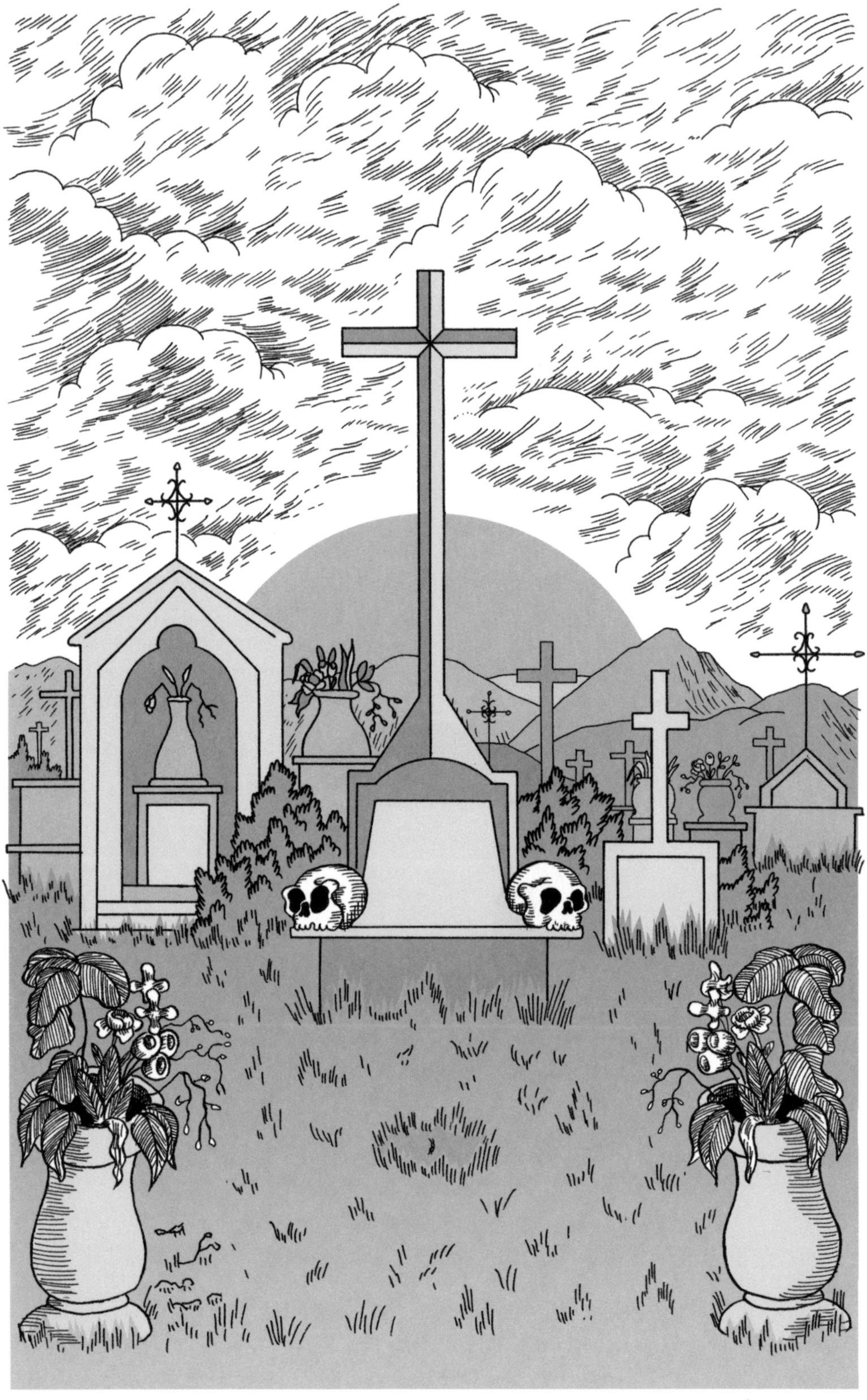

Martin mopes around the Messkirch cemetery, dragging his feet like a soul in distress. He's been like this ever since he was born. He wonders what he's doing here, in the world, and above all, why he's been thrown into it if only to die one day. He also wonders why things exist, since they will disappear as well. He even asks himself why he asks all these questions …

It is said that grouches, like all other bugs, cannot conceive their own death, that they are content to perish, just as flowers are content to wilt. But not our poor Martin!

At night, when darkness falls and all the familiar things are plunged into obscurity, when everything become silent, heavy, and strange, when the chest of drawers vanishes from his room, followed by the bed and then the table, he feels alone, terribly alone. And so he moans, "But why am I here?"

When he was only a little grouch, he couldn't shake off the threat of dying. He would imagine monsters under his bed, incredible thunderstorms, a cacophony of fears, then he would hide his head under the covers and call out for his parents— and they would soothe his distress … until the following night. For although the monsters disappeared, the possibility of dying never did …

Now that he is no longer a child, he has stopped hiding under the covers. But he has dreadful insomnia: with every fiber of his being, he feels that being there, thrown out into the world, is one very strange adventure.

From now on, he isn't scared anymore. He is anxious.

One winter morning after a particularly difficult night, Martin takes a stroll around the cemetery. A snail friend of his passes by and remarks, "What a terrible face you're making, Martin! Did something awful happen?"

"The worst of misfortunes, my dear Epicurus: I was born and I will die."

"Ah, you'll never change! Instead of wallowing in these musings, forge your way ahead, as I do!"

"How I would love to be carefree, my friend. What I wouldn't give to be like you."

"Nothing is easier! Tell yourself that while we are alive, death is not our concern, and when we are dead, we aren't around anymore to worry about it. So don't get yourself all upset; we all die one day!"

"Death is not our concern! We all die one day! You know, you've already fed me that line. But if you were to think seriously about death, you wouldn't say such things," moaned Martin.

"Oh, death, I know all about it! I can guarantee you that I've seen plenty of corpses. One of my cousins ended up in a jar, another was scalded, several of my relatives were suffocated by gas or burnt to a crisp, or eaten by crickets or birds ... I even saw half a dozen of my brothers cooked in garlic butter! In my family, the funerals are non-stop! So let me say it again: ONE dies one day and there's no point in making a big deal out of it!"

9

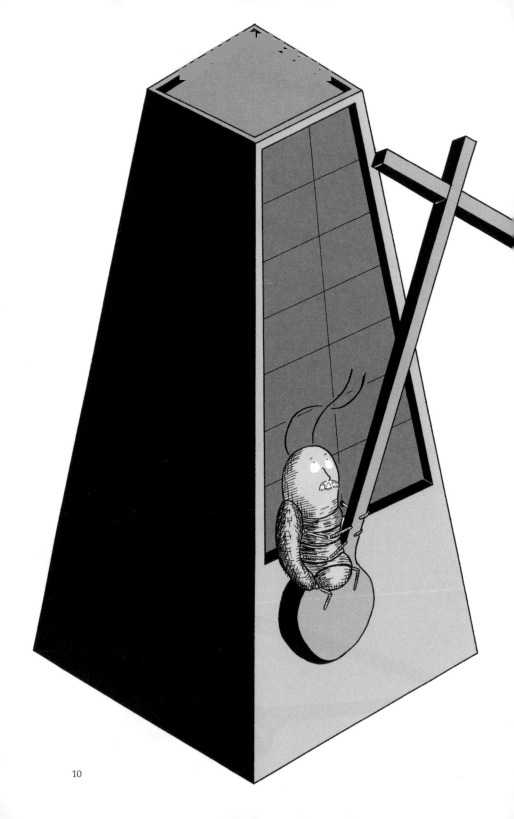

"ONE dies, ONE dies," exclaims Martin, "but it is not ONE who is going to die, but me! And not 'one day,' but perhaps tomorrow, perhaps today. Both of us are going to die, and even while I'm talking to you, in a certain sense we are moving towards death. I'm not talking about the carcases we find stuck to our shoe soles or in the special tongs used for eating snails: that is the death of others. Neither am I talking about the fact that all of us will kick the bucket sooner or later, but of the death that confronts us day and night from the inside and never lets up."

"Come now," says Epicurus, who is strangely feeling a bit down, "death is no big deal!"

"It's no big deal? Saying that does not reassure me for, in the end, perhaps it is existence that is 'no big deal.' Do you understand?"

"Well, uh ... of course, but I don't want to think like you," Epicurus says as he slides his head back into his shell. "I am young! I still have plenty of time ..."

"And yet, as soon as a snail is born, it is already old enough to die. Most people forget that and say: 'ONE dies.' But that is just a headlong attempt to escape. 'ONE dies' could mean me or another, a bit of everyone and no one who dies. But death is seeped into your shell, into my carapace, into human skin, into all who know they are mortal. What strange creatures we are, Epicurus! Here we are, we exist, but we know there will be an end."

"I don't want to hear anymore about it!" whined Epicurus, completely withdrawn into his shell.

Martin continues his gloomy rambling with his head bowed. "But what kind of being am I?" he murmurs. Suddenly, he hears a little voice say, "Here I am!"

Surprised, he looks around. He thinks he can just make out a little girl sitting on a tomb, but as he walks closer, he sees that it's a battery-operated doll, dropped and forgotten by some child. The dampness in the air must have caused a short circuit, for the doll keeps repeating over and over, "Here I am ... crrr ... Here I am ... crrr ..."

The grouch finds the situation rather funny, as the doll's mechanism can say, just like him, "Here I am." Nevertheless, he wouldn't say that the doll has been born into the world or that it exists.

"What am I," wonders Martin, "compared to this thing? I too can say, 'Here I am!' just like the doll. And yet I see a big difference. When the doll says, 'Here I am,' it is making noises, words, but it isn't speaking! It doesn't know that it is here or that it will disappear one day. If it knew such things, it wouldn't just lay there like that, like a lead weight at the bottom of a river, waiting for time to destroy it! It isn't even aware that it is lying on a tomb."

"On the other hand, as for myself, I know there is a tomb, I also know what it is used for, who it belongs to, and who made it. That is what it means to exist: not simply to be in the world, thrown there, like the tombstone or the doll, but to be open to the world and to others and to participate in my common surroundings ... Alas! This still doesn't tell me why I am here."

He feels the anxiety come rushing back, threatening to spill over. He even ends up asking himself why the world itself exists, for that matter. Everything around him starts blurring together and losing its coherence: the cemetery, the sky, the trees, himself. All becomes hideous. He runs off like some desperate vermin, until, at the far end of the cemetery close to the rose bushes, he passes a widow kneeling before a gravestone.
She is repeating, "He was such a great man! Such a great man!"

Intrigued, the grouch wonders to himself, "Ah ... a great one? I'll stop and watch a while, that will get my mind off my worries!"
The widow begins to read a poem in honor of her husband:
"Holy Greece! Home of all the gods ..."

The grouch rubs his front limbs together:
"He must have been a cultivated man! Learned men always have a slightly sugary taste that is not bad at all, like so much soft candy! First-rate cadaver. I'm going to fill my stomach; that will empty my head a bit!"

Martin lowers himself into the coffin, which is already cracked by the earth's shifting movements. What a disappointment! The man isn't great at all; he is even rather small. But he is rather paunchy. His flesh looks to be about medium rare. As he inspects the corpse laid out on satin, the grouch lets out a little groan, "And to think that I will end up in the same state!"

"By Jove," says a voice, "if I had known that insects make this much noise, I would have asked to be cremated. Normally, you aren't supposed to talk. Me neither, for that matter ..." Everybody knows that the deceased retain, for a short while, their habit of talking.

"Sorry for bothering you. I'll try to be quiet," Martin replies, his voice still cracking.

"That's alright," grumbles the cadaver. "But do I hear you sniffling? What's the matter? Normally, grubs and insects come in here a-singing, like bona fide cicadas on their way to a feast. Is my taste not to your liking?"

"Thank you for your concern, but I'm not feeling very well."

"I can't stand moaning, especially during meals. Tell me if I can help you. The dead are not as dull as you might think—they have plenty of time to ruminate."

"I seriously doubt there is anything you can say to make me feel better, for I am in the throes of agony. I am going to die. Consequently, I don't really understand why I exist."

"You couldn't be in better company! Let me tell you: I am a huge expert on this subject, a giant."

The grouch looks at the short body that thinks itself a giant.

"And to which giant do I have the honor of speaking?"

"I'm Heidegger. Hei-deg-ger. You've surely heard of me before? The philosopher ... the professor ... the author of *Being and Time* ..."

"*Bing-a-Dime*, never heard of it ... At any rate, I dare anyone to find a cure for my agony."

"A cure! Why do you want to find a cure? Dying is wonderful news. When you are dying, you feel utterly alone. Not even the person holding your hand to comfort you can share in this most personal experience. In the final instant, your solitude will be incredible! Can you feel it? Isn't it great? When I think seriously about my death, not others' death but my own, I feel deep inside of me how unique I am ... No one can die in MY place."

"I don't see how this is good news."

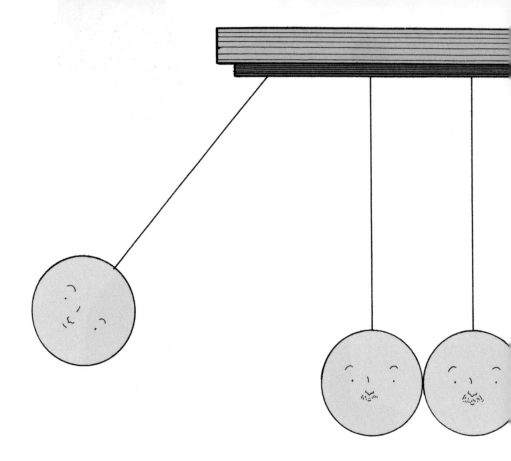

"Take my coffin, for example," Heidegger continues. "It is doomed to remain a coffin, limited to its function. As it has no consciousness of its use, it is there without trying to be anything else than a coffin designed to hold a body. It is fully realized as soon as it is built. But as for you, for as long as you exist, you will always be becoming. Nothing but death can bring you to completion. You are like a piece of fruit that is forever awaiting its ripening. This explains why you are always busy with some project, because death is the only end to existence. Yet in the meantime, one must live. We are creatures of care. I don't know what I have to do—I just feel that I must act. I don't know what I am, but I feel that I must be."

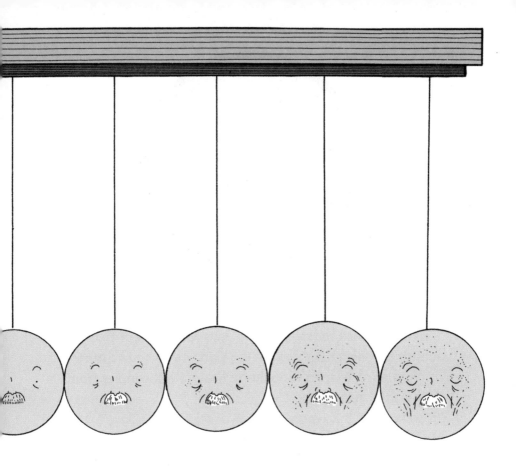

"But be what?"
"To be, that is all. You have an existence to make. And it's not
your neighbor's, it's yours, and no one can tell you how to
go about it."
Inside his shell, the grouch gets the chills. Suddenly he can
feel the weight of his miniscule self. For the first time he
doesn't think any more about the day of his death but about
all he can do on his way to death. After the chills he starts
to feel dizzy. That must be what real anxiety feels like! It's not
so much a problem of dying but of failing to live.

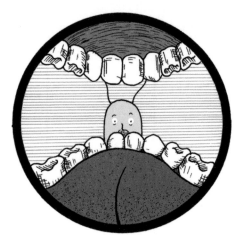

"I'm determined to live MY life," says Martin, "but that still doesn't tell me what I need to do. Can you give me a hint?"
In the silence, Martin thought he heard a call coming from the corpses' creases.
"It was a call! But who's calling?"
"I spent my whole life trying to give it a name, but the name never made it past the tip of my tongue," replies Heidegger.
Martin slips his head between the lips of the deceased.
"I can't see a thing!"
"Ffit's an expreffion."
"What I heard was so strange—I'd like to go see. Towards what should I head?"
"Towards nothing at all," replies Heidegger.
But Martin didn't listen to the late Heidegger. Consumed by curiosity, he continues past the half-circle of teeth. Was it really a call? He couldn't be sure because, once he thinks about it, he didn't actually hear any sound. It was more like an impression, some sort of unspoken invitation.

On his way down the esophagus, he passes an ant.

It appears to be at ease, totting a piece of straw on its shoulder.

"Are you the one who called me?" asks Martin.

"No, I didn't say anything. But what are you doing around here?"

"I'm not really sure. I'm looking for someone or something, so I'm checking around a bit. I'll grab a bite to eat on the go. This is quite a nice place," Martin remarks as he looks at his surroundings. "A very lovely throat."

"ONE couldn't wish for more. I am right where I belong."

Martin is very intrigued. The ant feels at home! "How does she manage?" he asks himself. Martin never feels at home.

"How fulfilled you seem ..."

"As much as an ant can be. I'm a worker ant: I wake up, I gather, I dig tunnels, I contribute to the ant-hill. During this time, soldiers guard the food reserves, and the queen governs and gives birth to soldiers or workers. I am useful to others, and other ants are useful to me—what more could you want? A real chain. Isn't this also the case for grouches?"

"Oh no, we're rather solitary bugs. Although we have a colony, each grouch just looks out for itself." Martin thinks it must be quite pleasant to be an ant. "Any chance there's a job opening for me in your ant-hill?" he asks.

"You'd have to see the queen about that. But follow me, we always need extra hands."

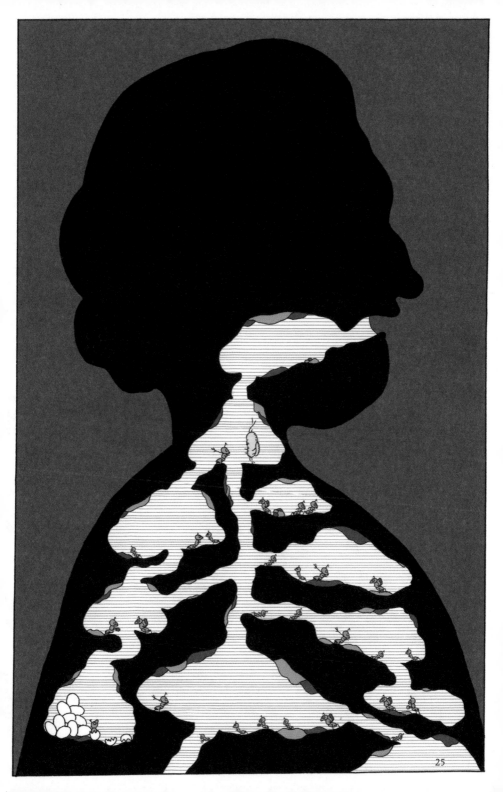

Martin follows close behind the worker ant: he crosses one, two, three ants, then finds himself in the middle of a crowd. He must be in a public area. What a lot of racket! ONE chatters away about one thing or another, pretending to be interested in what the ant next to them is saying without really listening. ONE talks about world affairs, local affairs, from far-away, from everywhere, from nowhere. ONE speaks of food shortages, of foreign ants who come to steal the crumbs from honest ants, but above all, ONE talks about the red ants, repeating with every breath, "I hate them. They are everywhere!" Then, suddenly, ONE falls silent. "The queen is about to speak," whispers Martin's guide. A deep black ant wearing a straw crown appears upon a balcony built into the breach of an ulcer.

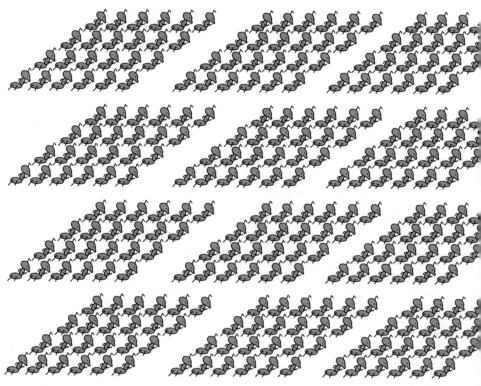

"Hail the Queen!" cry the ants, enraptured. "Our guiding light!"

They all line up, and to not get stepped on, Martin decides to follow the movement. One step to the left, another to the right ... left, right, left ... he finds himself enlisted into a column. He doesn't dare step out of line because he is afraid of being noticed, but also because he likes how it feels to be in the middle of a group. All these little creatures who march and cry out in unison "Long live the queen!" makes him shudder. Feeling upbeat, he thinks he has finally found a purpose for his existence: he would like to be a black ant, to pulsate with all the others at the same time.

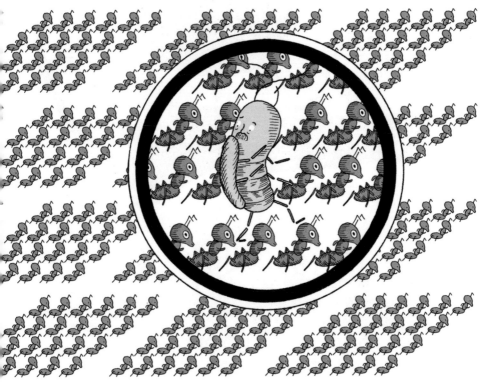

Total silence. Then the queen starts to yell like a lunatic! What energy! Martin is fascinated. "WE have an enemy," begins the queen, tapping her front limbs upon the ledge. "WE all know it! Before, WE were dying of hunger, WE had to hang our heads low, but today, WE know who is responsible for our misfortune: the red ants! We all know what ONE says about them, and yet that isn't the half of it! Above all ONE says that they are everywhere and that they work to our disadvantage. But to whom does the corpse of Heidegger belong? To them or to us?"

And all the ants applaud and acclaim their queen. They all say that she is right: ONE has indeed heard all these things about the red ants.

"We must use all our energy to push them back!" yells the queen, ever more hysterical, her eyes bulging out of her skull. "And everything among us, right down to the slightest blade of grass, must serve the homeland! The flesh of other insects is but soldier's rations! Our workers serve the homeland by fashioning weapons of war, while I will serve the homeland by producing not offspring but patriots. ONE must form one body if ONE wants to escape being enslaved by sub-insects!"

Suddenly, the queen stops talking and points at Martin from her balcony. "Well what have we here … a visitor! What are you doing here?"

"Uh well … I'm listening to you. I would really love to work for you!"

"Hmm … tell me, what do you think of the red ants?"

"The same as everyone else!"

All the ants applaud. "Even grouches, whom ONE knows to be wise, agree with us! Death to the reds!" hurls the queen. And Martin feels himself being carried along by the movement of the mass. He is pleased to be thought wise. And since being wise apparently means saying what the others want to hear, he starts hollering, "Down with the red ants! Long live the insects with a brown carapace!" He is a huge success. And so, to keep it up, he goes even further. He says that the red ants refuse to share and that they have many other, even worse faults. At any rate, that's what ONE says. The queen, delighted to welcome a new ally, orders that he be given a position in the Great Mechanism. Recognition, a job, fellow citizens, a homeland! Martin is beside himself with joy! He finally has a place in the world. Now he knows what he must be: an ant. And he knows what he must do: serve the ant-hill. And while Martin yells and raises his arms with the others, he feels, for the first time in his entire life perhaps, satisfied. How nice it is to fade into a crowd, to feel useful, to forget about the rest, and to no longer feel the torments of anxiety!

Martin is thrilled. He is led toward the Great Mechanism. He is so impatient that he starts to trot along! He asks himself what in the world it could be. Below, gastric juices flow in boiling waves. On the surface swim pieces of food that the recumbent statute did not have time to digest. The place is rather cozy. It feels like a good place to live. But as he gets closer, a noise grows louder and louder until it is downright deafening: limbs smacking, carapaces ramming into each other, jaws hacking. An entire battalion of ants hard at work! A real factory has been set up, with the stomach rumbling like that of an enormous giant.

So this is the Great Mechanism. It is orderly and impersonal. The force of the gastric juices is strong enough to turn a gigantic wheel. A conveyer belt is attached. Trays scrape away Heidegger's flesh and deposit their content into wicker tubs. Bit by bit, the cadaver is decomposed and stored away. The mechanism cuts, crushes, reduces, operates, pounds, distributes and begins again. The gears turn frenetically. What a racket! A foreman welcomes Martin. Over the noise of the gears, he hollers, "The queen sent word that you are to work in the Great Mechanism. I am going to show you your station." Martin, a little hesitant, follows him with a mixture of enthusiasm and dread.

The two insects enter the Great Mechanism. The sight is astonishing. Industriously, the bugs scamper, exchange orders, spread open blueprints, measure, survey, and gauge the deceased's body. Some bend beneath the weight of huge tubs, their six legs compressed into the ground. Pointing to an ant who looks wiped out, the foreman tells Martin, "Your job will be to motivate the workers. They must keep up the pace and sacrifice themselves for the ant-hill."

"Well how am I supposed to do that? What am I supposed to say?"

"I haven't the slightest idea! Use your imagination! Tell them ONE must serve the ant-hill because the ant-hill serves the ants."

Martin begins his job rather cleverly, it must be said. He speaks about the ant-hill's destiny. He tries to arouse a patriotic spirit so that the ants will accomplish their tasks with zeal. He even tries to get them to understand that the meaning of their existence lies in their collective submission to the queen. Martin feels useful. He believes that he will help others find meaning for their lives. But one day, as he inspects the innermost recess of the factory, he discovers the lot reserved for the red ants.

They are so thin that even their carapace looks too big for
them. They appear to be neither dead nor alive.

From this day on, Martin loses heart in his work. He finally goes to see the foreman. "I would like to quit," he says. "Here no one quits. What fault do you find with your labor?" "Not a thing. Everything works perfectly. It would take my colony years to extract so much food. But there is something alarming about this system."

"What is alarming about it?" the foreman asks Martin.

"Good old Heidegger is here for us to consume. And so we help ourselves. The gastric juices are useful in turning the power station, activates the excavators, which dig the flesh, which is then loaded into the tubs. The wind serves to protect the winged ants, the ground to protect our larva, and Heidegger's corpse is calculated to provide us with meat. The workers do their work and if ever any of them are no longer useful, ONE throws them in a corner where they will be devoured later. Where's the problem? There is nothing alarming about this system. To the contrary, it guarantees us a radiant future!"

"But there are also the red ants! To consider Heidegger an available food reserve is one thing, but do you really have the right to exploit the others?"

"Everyone must serve."

"But what you are doing is insecticide! It doesn't make sense to me."

"Er, well, it's useful for the ants!"

"In that case, I no longer see the usefulness of the ant ..."

"The usefulness of the ant is the ant, and that is that."

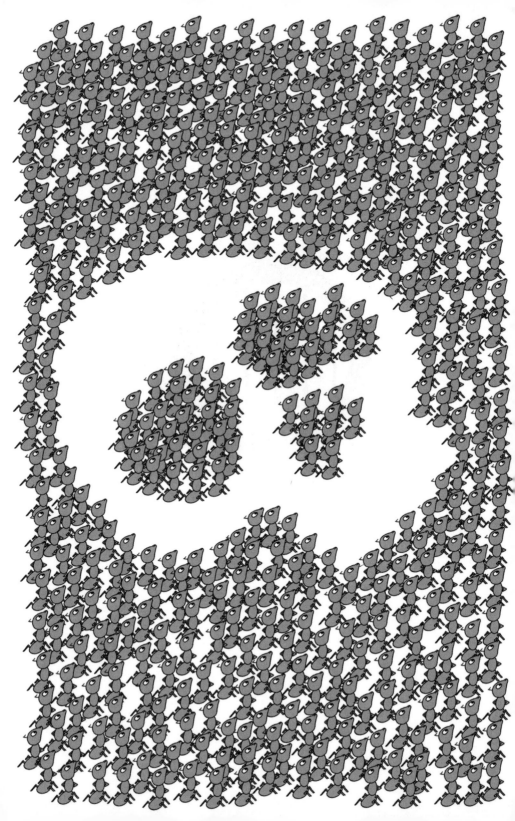

"'The goal of the ant is the ant!' What a clever reply!"
exclaims Martin. "You remind me of those dogs that chase
their own tail. That gets you nowhere."
"Now see here!" thunders the foreman, who doesn't
know how one is supposed to respond to such challenges.
"Everyone else does it like we do it, and we do it like
everyone else."
"But who tells you that everyone else does it like you?"
"Everyone."
"But who is this everyone?"
"It is what ONE says, that is all. ONE hears it everywhere."
"Come now, those are empty words. Who is this ONE who
gives you so many certainties?"
"It's a little bit each ant, and all ants at the same time.
It's what ONE says."
"But who saw what ONE says, who gave you these ideas?
Tell me! No one! These are ONE-says ideas, what one must
say to be well-accepted by the black ants. 'And the red ants
this, and the black ants that, and the Great Mechanism is
ingenious, and efficient, and blah blah blah.' In short, it's
empty chatter. ONE tries to busy one's mind, and that gives
it something to chew on in conversations, but in the end, the
words are empty. If everyone ended up behaving like everyone
else, ONE would no longer know who thinks what! I'm sorry,
but following the commands of the people, of the Queen,
and of the ONE-says is not what it means to live one's OWN
life!"

"I detest your view of the world," hisses the foreman.
"But this isn't a view of the world—I'm not pretending to
know the truth. I'm just saying that the black ants are being
taken for a strange ride. Each one believes that the others
know the destination, but in fact everyone just follows each
other, hurtling along, without really knowing where they
are going. The entire ant-hill follows the dictates of ONE-
says. And if you're still going to say that all your actions are
the most useful ones, then please tell me what's the
use of usefulness!"

Before the grouch could finish his sentence, the foreman
spurts a jet of acid at him.

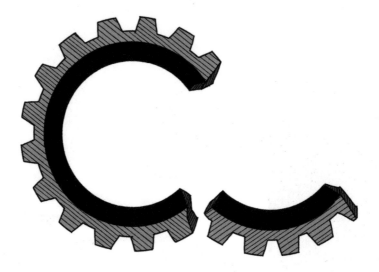

Martin starts running to get away and jumps into the waves
of bile. He grabs on as best he can to a candied cherry that
probably used to decorate a chocolate pastry. The soldiers,
alerted by the foreman's hollering, march back and forth upon
the embankment. The grouch drifts further and further away
from the ants' frantic hustling and bustling. He clutches onto
a piece of radish, then an apple seed, and drifts for a while on
a wilted leaf of lettuce ... He floats in the comforting silence
of Martin Heidegger's body, far from the miniature society of
pipsqueaks with their noisy and gleamingly modern constructions.
Far from the acid and the insults, far from the swarming
movements of ONE-says.

Suddenly the small raft gets caught in an eddy. The current accelerates, pulling Martin along. Luckily, before being sucked down, he manages to grab onto the opposite shore.

Martin hoists himself up onto the embankment. He can't believe he let himself get caught up in the ants' game. He's terribly upset at himself for having aided and abetted such fanatics. He stretches out and waits for his tiny wings to dry a little. He is under a sky of ribs and steeped in the delicious stench of decomposition: the heaps of flesh, the dried blood, the fat cells and the bushes of capillary vessels surround him like so many eerie trees. "Decidedly, everything I attempt thrusts me into an inauthentic existence! So what is there left for me to do to become myself? Must I roam, again and forever, in pursuit of an answer?" While probing his consciousness and his failings, he wanders deeper and deeper into a strange forest; He tangles his foot in a clump of roots, hits his head on low-hanging branches, and gets lost in the dark shadows. Nature in all her glory enfolds him: secret, monstrous, nearly repugnant.

Finally, the world opens before him once more as he reaches a clearing flooded with light.

What a relief! In the middle of the bright light, he sees
a little group of worms squirming together listlessly. They are
glistening, magnificent, serene; their rings rub against each
other in silence. Suddenly, one of them lifts its head and asks,
"Who goes there? A friend?" The blind worm doesn't know
in which direction to lean his head to catch the reply.
"A friend," says Martin.
"You seem quite out of breath. Where do you come from?"
"I was in the ant-hill, where I had a terrible experience!"
"But where the danger is, also grows the saving power,"
quotes another worm, raising his head. Martin's eyes widen.
"Bravo, my dear Friedrich," the worm says to his friend.
"But you," he asks Martin, "what did you come here for?"
"An answer to the question: 'Why am I here?' But I doubt
you can help me."
"The rose is without why; it blooms because it blooms,
It pays no attention to itself, asks not whether it is seen,"
chants another worm, cheered on by the others.
"Well said, Silesius!"

"You'll have to excuse me," says the grouch, annoyed by all these enigmas. "You're confusing me! If there's no reason to my being here, then I might as well throw myself down the drain!" Another worm starts to speak, "Lucidity is the wound closest to the sun." His companions utter cries of admiration, "Magnificent, René!" As for Martin, he simply sighs.

"We were like you are before we entered Heidegger," says the worm. "WE were content to wriggle around and to feed ourselves, happy enough until the food was completely gone, then WE took off blindly in search of another meal. But here, we have learned to see ..."

"To see what?" asks the grouch, rubbing his antennas together.

"Most folks prefer to believe that the goal of existence is to serve their homeland, their family, their economy, but also to serve themselves, to consume. And yet they feel an emptiness. Every day, they tell themselves, 'No, to exist cannot be only this ...' But almost immediately, they try to forget what they just said."

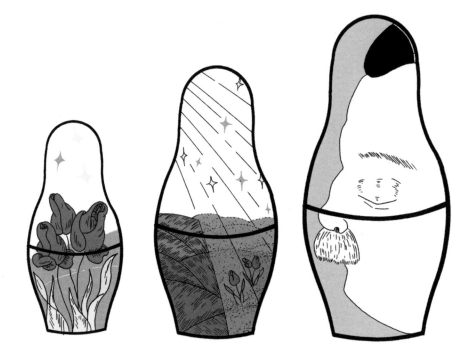

"And so, rather than use empty words, worn out by everyone who says them, we prefer to render thanks to what is around us, by saying, for example, 'The lone flowers open in the prairie.'" As he hears these words, Martin notices the little blood-hued flowers that are open pretty much all over the clearing. He hadn't paid attention any to them, and yet they were there before he arrived. "You see these flowers," continued the worm, "they wouldn't be here without the clearing. You can thank Heidegger's corpse for being there, since without him, you wouldn't have seen the clearing. Thank also the cemetery, for without it, the body wouldn't have found a shelter, and above all, thank the other shelter, the vast one, for without it you wouldn't have seen anything at all."

"What shelter are you talking about?"

"Well, I mean ... the world!"

"But I can't see it or say what it is," murmurs Martin, "so how can I thank it?"

"Now you've got it," whispers the worm mischievously. "The world shines by its absence. You don't see it, you don't hear it, you don't feel it, and yet it harbors everything you see! It compels you to find the words to say it. Here is our task: to dwell poetically in the world."

"But that doesn't make any sense!" Martin says, a bit worriedly. "If no one can hear it or see it, finding words to speak the world is pointless!"

"Be silent, look around, and you will hear its call."

"The head whizzes through the galaxy of the absurd," René sings out before slinking back among his peers. Martin scrutinizes the Heideggerian vault. He still doesn't see anything but food, and he wonders how many pounds it all weighs, how many colonies could be fed by this supply. Then he tries to look beyond what is merely useful. And suddenly, he sees!

A richer world opens to him. He notices the interlacing of shadow and light, and he feels the bumps and hollows of the ground. When one takes the time to look at him, Heidegger is rather lovely when seen no longer as a buffet but for what he is ... A tangibly mountainous landscape with passes, summits, and valleys. His tendons that hang like ivy. This is what he should have shown to the world-impoverished ants. They needed to be snatched away from their factory and taken on a trip: by boat, by ski, or simply on foot.

He keeps looking and notices that the ribs create a white framework. They hold back a mass of flesh that resembles a stormy sky traced with flashes of lightening. Martin hadn't paid attention to that. And yet it's something worth seeing, something truly beautiful. For those who know how to look at things, the flesh is not only meat to be harvested by the Great Mechanism, nor only a territory to be conquered; it has form, color, taste, and weight, and a certain level of humidity.
It makes noise, its gases sputter and smell, its odor mixes with that of the soil, and inside this subtle combination drifts the scent of decomposing clothes. In sum, if a body stops being used, the entire world emerges gently within it.

"I can't find the words to say what I feel," groans the grouch, "I feel overwhelmed, torn open towards something I do not grasp."
"That is what it means to exist, my friend!"
Martin racks his brain. He studies everything in the clearing:
"The meat features hints of purple," he says after a long moment of meditation.
"Not bad!" laughs the worm.
"The roots tickle the earth's chest."
"Better and better!"
"Heidegger's head in sticky sap! How exciting it is to get carried away!" Martin exclaims. "Quite a difference from the rote phrases of ONE-says."

Martin thanks the brilliant messengers before plunging back into the cadaver's crevasses. He explores every single nook and cranny. Having thought that to exist was to roam, he now understands that it is in fact a trip. Having arrived at the edge of the kidneys, he contemplates the hues of the flesh, enjoying the pungent smell and the purple tinges. The things that he sees, feels, and hears are all different and yet, he knows they have something in common because they are there, in the same world.

"If I must come up with an answer, then I would say that what things have in common must itself be different from all things, or else it would just be one thing among others. How to name this difference that allows things to be present without itself being present? This element that escapes me, that I will never see or touch or manage to name perfectly, but that nevertheless makes itself heard and calls out to me, what shall I name it? That which allows us to call something this or that, such is the source of all that is present, and I could no doubt call it being."

"Here is the meaning of my existence: to ask myself the question of being without ceasing, to avoid giving answers to the goal of existence like the Queen or the foreman did. Why are there things, what is the purpose of my existence? All these tasks that must be undertaken before dying without any hope of ever accomplishing them. What anxiety, what anxiety! But ... The joy of living hits me like a thunderbolt. I can't wait to share my discovery with Epicurus!"

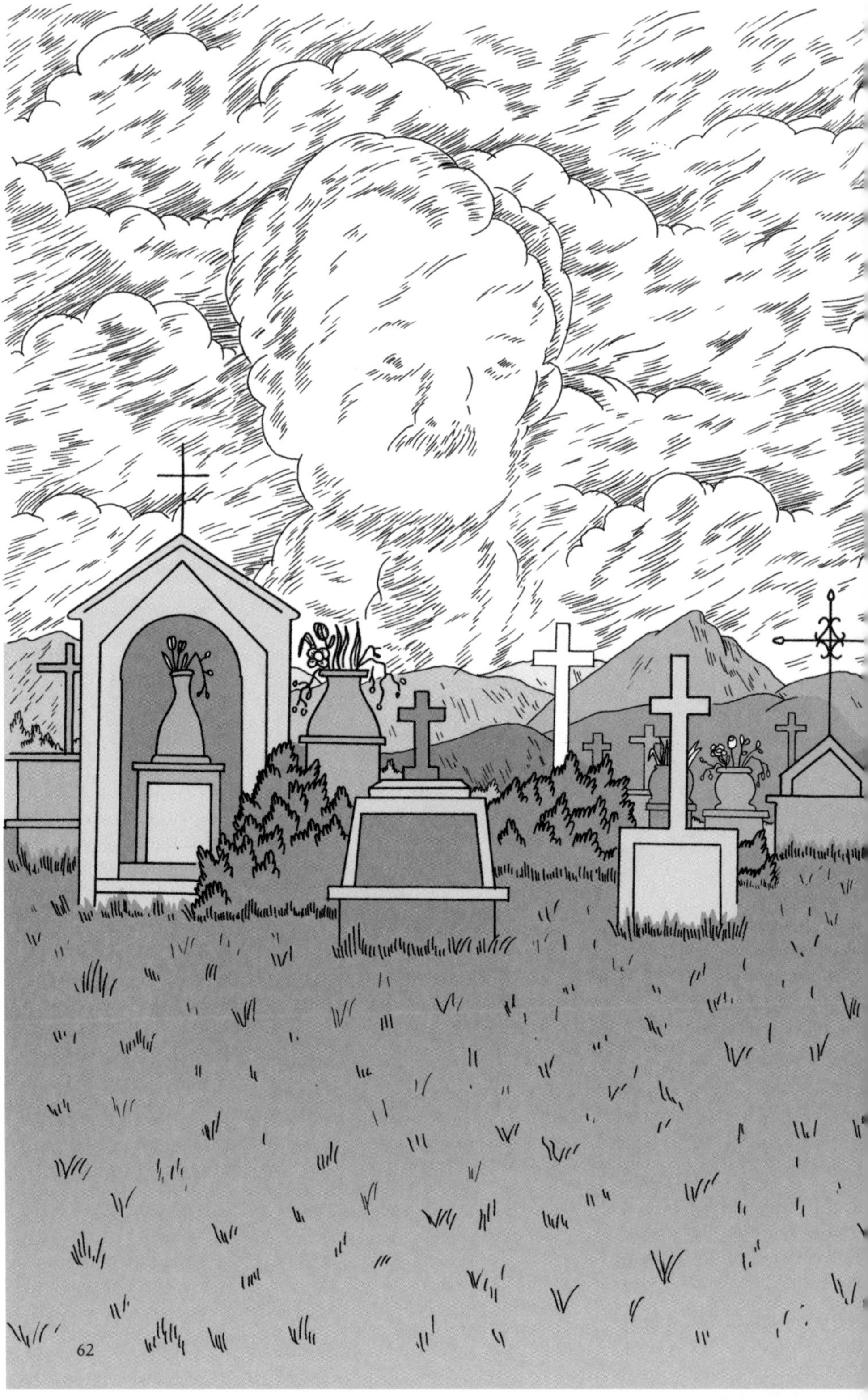

Back up on the surface, Heidegger's widow can't believe her ears. In the silence of this garden of death, could that be a little voice singing, astonished at itself, radiant?

Martin Heidegger
1889—1976
To follow a star
Only this

French edition:

Yan Marchand & Matthias Arégui

Le Cafard de Martin Heidegger

Design: Yohanna Nguyen

© Les petits Platons, Paris 2011

First edition

ISBN 978-3-0358-0052-4

© diaphanes, Zurich 2018

www.diaphanes.com

Layout: 2edit, Zurich

Printed and bound in Germany